Below: *The Edinburgh Military Tattoo transforms the Castle Esplanade at Festival time each year*

MW01687280

in 1991

To theatre and history must be added another strand. Edinburgh's citizens consider their city to be a very cosmopolitan place. Certainly, its visitors come from all over the world, and not only at Festival time. Its cuisine and the international hotel chains which are present in the city centre confirm this. Away from the visitors, behind the scenes, perhaps in discreet offices in city-centre streets such as Charlotte Square, its financial institutions handle enough business to make Edinburgh the second largest financial centre in the UK. More than 200 years ago, during the century in which Scotland lost its independence, Edinburgh, capital of the nation, instead of losing its way, became a centre of excellence in a great advance of the arts and sciences which became known as the Age of Enlightenment. Today at schools and universities, as well as in such bodies as the Royal Society of Edinburgh, the aspirations of those days echo still. Thus, though the outward face of Edinburgh makes an immediate impact on the visitor, there is much more to this city than simply a dramatic skyline.

Below: *Edinburgh from Arthur's Seat, looking north across the Firth of Forth to Fife*

The origins of Edinburgh

Archaeological excavation work as recently as 1989 has pushed back the earliest-known occupancy date for the Castle Rock, the dramatic crag on which today's fortifications stand, far beyond the previous estimates of many authorities. It had been suggested that the site was used in the Dark Ages (around AD 600) as a hill fort. During excavation undertaken prior to re-development as part of an improvement to visitor facilities, archaeologists found evidence of an Iron Age fort. Within it was the site of an Iron Age house (itself around AD 100) and, at the very lowest level were found fragments of pottery and chewed herring-bones from the Bronze Age. Radiocarbon analysis of this very early sample of Edinburgh's cuisine suggested a date of about 800 BC.

Long before even the first hunter-gatherers made their way along the shores of the Firth of Forth, a glacier had ground its way eastwards, round the hard volcanic material of the Castle Rock, to form steep faces on three sides, while the fourth became a 'tail' or ramp of material which ran downhill and eastwards for a mile. This crag and tail, as described by geologists, formed the basis of the settlement - a cluster of primitive dwellings in the shadow and shelter of a protecting fortress. Excavations have revealed traces of the early castle structures - the Iron Age fort has long disappeared from view. In fact nothing really survives from those early times. Not until the eleventh century does the story of Edinburgh and its castle become anything more than conjecture.

Queen Margaret, the southern Saxon queen of the Scots king Malcolm III (Malcolm

Below: *St Margaret's Chapel, the oldest building in Edinburgh.* **Bottom:** *Princes Street from the castle, looking across Princes Street Gardens to the New Town*

Canmore), persuaded her husband to move his court from Dunfermline to Edinburgh. It is said she found the Lothians, for long ruled by Saxon Northumbrians rather than northern Celts, more to her taste. At that time the main building of the castle stood behind wooden defences. It was high on the Castle Rock that the saintly Queen Margaret had built Edinburgh's oldest surviving structure, now known as St Margaret's Chapel. Her son, King David I was involved in another basic feature of the shape of early Edinburgh. He founded Holyrood Abbey, from which today's Palace of Holyroodhouse gradually evolved.

As for the various castle buildings erected over the centuries, none except St Margaret's Chapel survived, for a variety of military reasons. All were, for example, destroyed in 1314 by Randolph, Earl of Moray, so that the castle could not be defended should it again fall into English hands during the Scots wars of independence. Further substantial alterations took place after a great siege in 1571, when Kirkcaldy of Grange and his forces held the castle for Mary Queen of Scots after she had abandoned the Scottish throne. The siege, carried out by the Regent Morton, finally led to the surrender of the defenders, but only after substantial damage by cannon fire had all but demolished major parts of the fortress. The conspicuous Half-Moon Battery (so named from its shape) was built subsequent to this most damaging episode in the castle's story. Cromwell took the castle in 1650, after another siege had first battered it by cannon. Further minor battles led to various defensive improvements.

Even these brief glimpses of military activity centred around Edinburgh Castle show how the site evolved through the years. Today, the castle still has substantial military presence, though its main points of interest are varied and include the Scottish Regalia, in the Crown Room. These comprise the crown, sceptre and sword of the Scottish monarchy, hidden away in 1707 when Scotland gave up her sovereignty, until a search instigated by Sir Walter Scott discovered them in a dusty trunk in 1818. Now they have pride of place. Another famous artefact on display is the fifteenth-century cannon, Mons Meg. (It is not this military piece which fires the 'one o'clock gun' - a daily time-check guaranteed to startle visitors anywhere in the vicinity of the castle ramparts or Princes Street Gardens.)

The Scottish National War Memorial and the Scottish United Services Museum are reminders of the symbolic role of Edinburgh Castle as the heart of Scotland. The Great Hall is likewise full of historical interest, and the royal apartments include the tiny room in which Mary Queen of Scots gave birth to the future King James VI.

Below: *Edinburgh's walls and gates*

Right: *Edinburgh Castle from the Grassmarket.*
Bottom right: *Edinburgh Castle from Victoria Street, a Victorian development which altered the original main route up to the Castle Rock*

The Old Town

Edinburgh Castle, the Palace of Holyroodhouse and a sloping ridge between - these were the basic ingredients of the shape of old Edinburgh - the sloping ridge became the backbone of the Royal Mile, with the castle at its head. Little closes, or alleyways, run off the main thoroughfare like ribs. At the foot of today's High Street, where the road narrows just below the building known as John Knox's House, and where St Mary's Street meets the High Street, the Netherbow Port used to stand. Port here means 'gate' and today's visitors can see a plaque on which is drawn the shape of the old town gate which gave access to the east. This spot, about half a mile from the castle entrance, represented the most easterly point of the town walls by the sixteenth century.

Before the Scots were defeated at Flodden in 1513 (and in consequence started a new wall, fearing their capital vulnerable), an earlier set of defences, known as the King's Wall, took in an even smaller area. By the time what became known as the Flodden Wall was built (1514-60), the area occupied by the capital was contained within a boundary which ran south from the Castle Rock to just beyond the Grassmarket, then east, taking in Greyfriars Church, then continuing through today's Royal Museum of Scotland, in Chambers Street, as far as the foot of Drummond Street. There it met the old street, once a main route out of Edinburgh to the south, still known as the Pleasance. It is in this area that the best-preserved portions of town wall survive. Hereabouts the wall ran north, towards the site of Waverley Station, where it turned into the deep

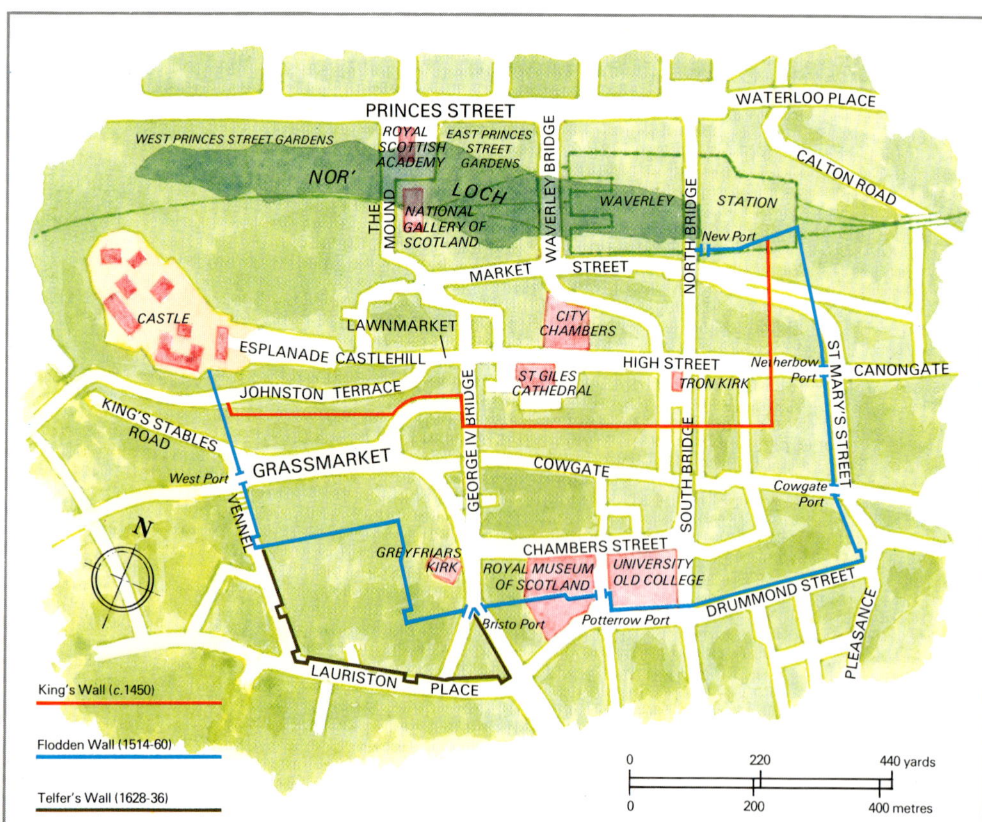

valley between Princes Street and the castle. Another line of defence took over here, though it has now vanished completely. This was the Nor' Loch, at various times loch or marsh, artificially dammed and maintained to make a defence for the city from the north.

Remember that this description was of the extended defences, the Flodden Wall. The earlier King's Wall, built around 1450, ran eastwards, parallel to the High Street but only 100 metres or so from it. Truly, Edinburgh in the Middle Ages

The Edinburgh Woollen Mill

Left: *John Knox's House. Popular sentiment - because of its association with the fiery preacher, John Knox - saved this sixteenth-century building from redevelopment in the nineteenth century*

Bottom left: *The Tolbooth, which was swept aside in the early part of the nineteenth century.*
Below: *Gladstone's Land, now in the care of the National Trust for Scotland, gives a hint of seventeenth-century life on the Royal Mile*

and even later was tiny by today's standards. As the town expanded within its confines, it was forced to grow upwards. Typical High Street buildings from those early days have been mostly swept aside, but a few survivors indicate what the Old Town must have been like. Tall tenements, or 'lands', in stone gradually evolved from the first wooden buildings. John Knox's House and its neighbour Moubray House, at the foot of the High Street, hint at the Old Town's sixteenth-century appearance. Projecting wooden galleries at first-floor level - surviving uniquely in John Knox's House - would have made the narrow street gloomy and canyon-like. A little later, the emphasis became thoroughly vertical. When, in 1617, a certain Thomas Gledstanes bought another sixteenth-century building further up the Royal Mile, in the Lawnmarket, he soon altered it. He removed the wooden gallery and instead created an arcaded stone front. This high tenement today survives in the care of the National Trust for Scotland and is known as Gladstone's Land, a flavour of typical seventeenth-century architecture. Thus the buildings in the Old Town evolved through the centuries to make the interesting mix of today.

As a place of organised commerce, Edinburgh developed early. In a charter of 1128, King David I refers to the place as a burgh - a Scottish term essentially meaning a community with trading rights, allowed to hold fairs and markets and able to charge tolls and levies. Some of these were remitted to the King, and some were used within the community. The symbols of burgh life in Edinburgh, and in other parts of Scotland were (in addition to the kirk): the Tolbooth or Town House (serving as an administrative centre, town council meeting-place, court of justice and prison) and also the Mercat Cross, the symbolic heart of the town, where royal proclamations were read and where the townsfolk and merchants would assemble. The city of Edinburgh today has lost its Tolbooth, demolished in 1817, but its Mercat Cross still stands below the High Kirk of St Giles.

Below the High Street, beyond what would

have been the Old Town walls, the Royal Mile is still called the Canongate (that is, the street of the canons, or monks, who were part of Holyrood Abbey). The Canongate actually existed as a burgh independent from Edinburgh until it was incorporated into the city, as recently as 1856. Proof of this is seen today in the form of its own surviving tolbooth. For centuries the community of the Canongate grew to meet the needs of the abbey below, in an exact parallel to the growth of its grand neighbour up the hill and behind the wall, which served the needs of the castle.

By the sixteenth century, Edinburgh had started to spill off the ridge of the Royal Mile. The buildings on the Royal Mile itself grew even taller, the castle became more extensive and the royal palace was made grander. In the eighteenth century other European cities were spreading in area and being rebuilt in the style of the Neo-classical Age. Cramped and confined, the Old Town of Edinburgh was forced to consider its future.

TOLBOOTH TAVERN

Left: *The Canongate Tolbooth, once the administrative centre of the independent burgh of the Canongate, is now a City Museum*

Below: *Part of the Old Town from Princes Street Gardens. In the centre is the Assembly Hall, meeting-place of the General Assembly of the Church of Scotland*

However, before condemning the Old Town for its cramped situation and inevitably insanitary conditions, it should be noted that this very closeness of the community brought with it certain advantages. By the middle of the eighteenth century, Edinburgh was the winter residence of many of the wealthier Scottish landowners, men of power and influence, who met and mingled with their cousins, perhaps lawyers, ministers or medical men - well travelled on the Continent - intellectuals who had probably taken courses at European universities. All lived in close proximity to each other in the tall tenement blocks of the Royal Mile - as did the ordinary folk of Edinburgh. Traditionally, the better off, for example, the judges or aristocracy, inhabited the middle reaches of the buildings - just high enough to escape the smelly streets below, but not so high as to make the climb to their premises tiring. There they were sandwiched between the 'other ranks'. However, in this setting, a cross-fertilisation of ideas took place. The novelist Tobias Smollett, in his novel *Humphrey Clinker* made the famous remark, 'Edinburgh is a hotbed of genius.' An observation made by a Mr Amyat, King's Chemist, and recorded by the printer, antiquarian and biographer, William Smellie, gives a further example of the unique circumstances in Edinburgh at that time: 'Here I stand at what is called the Cross of Edinburgh, and can, in a few minutes, take fifty men of genius and learning by the hand.'

The New Town in the Age of Enlightenment

George Drummond was an eighteenth-century Edinburgh citizen of the most public-spirited kind. He fought at the battle of Sheriffmuir in 1715 against the rebel Jacobites and took an anti-Jacobite stance thereafter. He served within the city as a councillor, baillie and treasurer, and was elected provost (equivalent to mayor in England) six times in all. He was active in the planning and building of what has been described as the city's first eighteenth-century building, formerly the Royal Exchange, now the City Chambers. Drummond was also a tireless champion of Edinburgh University and helped raise funds for the city's first infirmary. But amidst much good work and public service, he cherished a special dream: one which was admittedly shared by others and had been talked over for decades within the city. This was the creation of a new town of Edinburgh.

The story is told that Drummond looked out one day from a north-facing high window somewhere in the Old Town tenements. He gazed over the bare fields that climbed from the Nor' Loch onto a broad ridge before falling gradually towards the widening estuary of the River Forth at Leith, Edinburgh's seaport. Then he remarked to a companion standing with him, 'You are a young man and may probably live to see all these fields covered with houses, forming a splendid and magnificent city.'

Drummond eventually persuaded the less enthusiastic of his Town Council colleagues to authorise work on a means of making access easier to the broad ridge to the north. The foundation stone was laid of the first North Bridge, the predecessor of the bridge which carries today's traffic over the rooftops of Waverley Station and down to the east end of Princes Street. By 1766, a competition had been organised, inviting submissions for a plan for this new town. Unhappily within two months of the winning entry having been agreed, Drummond died, at the age of almost eighty years.

The winning scheme was the work of a

Below: *Edinburgh from the air, showing the Castle Rock with its steep crag and 'tail' or ramp running eastwards (right) on which the Old Town was built, as well as (centre and left) the New Town*

Below: *Calton Hill, where James Craig's Old Observatory stands, has an extraordinary collection of monuments, which add drama to the skyline of Edinburgh*

Right: *James Craig, winner of the competition to design the first New Town of Edinburgh*

twenty-three-year-old, more-or-less-unknown architect, James Craig. As a means of laying out streets on a hilltop piece of ground falling away from an east-west axis, Craig's plan had at least the merit of simplicity. Thus the first New Town was conceived as three parallel streets of which George Street was the highest and the centre, topped and tailed by a square at both east and west ends. The outermost streets, Princes Street and Queen Street would each overlook pleasure gardens: the former having castle views, the latter an open vista to the Forth estuary.

Craig's only surviving building within Edinburgh is the Old Observatory on Calton Hill. He did not actually design any of the structures in the first phase of the New Town; his prize-winning effort involved only the street plan. He also had an idea for the Nor' Loch's conversion into an ornamental canal, but though the shape of his New Town was eventually built, the canal was never constructed. In the next century this was to become the route eventually (after much opposition) taken by the railway. Perhaps the cleverest aspect of Craig's plan which was, it has to be remembered, for a residential area, was to propose that shops and services would be situated in two 'lesser' streets, Thistle Street and Rose Street, between the three grand and broad thoroughfares.

The name 'Princes Street' came about because King George III, to whom the plan was dedicated, did not like the original proposal, which was to call the street 'St Giles Street'. The King felt it reminded him of the St Giles area of London, in England, which had an infamous reputation. Instead he proposed 'Prince's Street' after the Prince Regent. In 1848 the plural form of 'Princes' was adopted and the apostrophe was abandoned altogether.

Today, though the most spectacular views of the southerly portion of the New Town are from the ramparts of Edinburgh Castle, it is also

Below: *The Mound (centre) and Princes Street from Edinburgh Castle. On the extreme right is North Bridge, the other main link between Old Town and New*

Right: *Edinburgh Castle from the Scott Monument. Only fit visitors will manage this view of Edinburgh!*

from this high viewpoint that it becomes most obvious how the character of Princes Street has changed. By the early years of the nineteenth century, commercial and retail operators were moving in, so that by the late twentieth century, Princes Street still has one of the most impressive settings of any street worldwide, but the quality of its architecture, housing high street multiples and retail developments, most people would consider fairly mixed.

The first house of Princes Street was completed in 1769, at about the same time as the new North Bridge, which meant that it was possible to cross from the Old Town to the site of the New Town dryshod. Many a worthy gentleman of the Old Town, on a mission to inspect, perhaps, his grand New Town house under construction, must have cursed the still improperly drained Nor' Loch as he slithered in the muddy valley bottom. At least two men must have done so. One was a clothier called George Boyd. He did not wish to leave the cosy, if cramped, conditions of the Old Town, where he had a shop in the Lawnmarket, but he was nevertheless conscious of the fact that the drift across the valley could adversely affect his business. The other gentleman was Baillie John Grieve, who had made the move to the fashionable part of town, but because of his involvement in the Town Council had to 'commute' between New Town and Old Town to attend meetings. Thus when George Boyd, with some friends, started piling earth and rubble to form a rough causeway across the mire of the Nor' Loch, John Grieve joined in. He initiated the moving of excavated material from buildings nearby and the dumping of it on the rough causeway. Soon, everyone agreed that this was a good idea, and the structure called 'Geordie Boyd's Mud Brig' or sometimes 'Baillie Grieve's Brig' soon became an earthen mound. By 1830, two million cart loads of earth later - or so the estimate goes - the carriageway now called the Mound was completed, to make the most direct link between the Old and New Towns.

Meanwhile, amidst all this frenzy of building work, while palace-fronted dwellings rose in symmetrical grandeur and locally quarried honey-coloured sandstone was painstakingly carved into pillars to carry the pediments of institutions such as the Royal Scottish Academy (at the corner of Princes Street and the Mound), there was another movement going on. This fine New Town would be the very symbol of Edinburgh's Age of Enlightenment - a realisation, too, of a new political stability in the latter half of

CEMETERY
FOR
SOLDIERS
DOGS

VWG 472Y

Left: *Royal Terrace. This is the longest continuous façade in the New Town of Edinburgh. Unfortunately it faces north, and it never acquired quite such an 'exclusive' tag as some of the earlier New Town developments*

Bottom left: *Dean Village lies only a few minutes' walk from Princes Street, yet its leafy walkways by the Water of Leith seem a world away from the busy city centre.* **Below:** *Moray Place, one of the most handsome streets in the New Town*

the eighteenth century. As far as the Scots could see, the future involved (whether the ordinary folk liked it or not) a united Britain and rule by the House of Hanover. The Jacobite bogeyman, after the defeat of Prince Charles Edward Stuart's forces at Culloden, had gradually receded.

All of the enlightened Scots' aspirations were embodied in the New Town: originally there were to be no shops and markets in the area; it was intended to be dedicated to the arts and learning. After the North Bridge was built and Craig's plan for Princes Street, George Street and Queen Street had been carried out, the success of the development generated further extensions: the well-known architect WH Playfair proposed a scheme for a further New Town beyond Calton Hill (at the east end of Princes Street) and stretching down towards Leith. This was at least partly built, and includes Royal Terrace, the longest continuous façade of the New Town, though this part of town never attained the same heights of desirability as other areas. Further extensions by Reid and Sibbald took Edinburgh down the slope from Queen Street towards the Water of Leith. Then the painter, Raeburn, added a little community development, almost out in the country, beyond the Water of Leith around Stockbridge. This included Ann Street, named after his wife, notable for its front gardens - an unusual New Town feature - and notable also for the asking prices for its properties today. Finally, and possibly amongst the most harmonious and magnificent, there was the Earl of Moray's development of the lands of Drumsheugh, which includes the much admired elevation of Moray Place.

Meanwhile, splendid public buildings also rose - not only the Royal Exchange in the Old Town, but also such works as Robert Adam's Register House, at the east end of Princes Street, built as a repository for the nation's records; and Edinburgh University's Old College building, south of the Old Town, as well as the National Gallery, both by Playfair. With these and other fine edifices, Edinburgh's reputation as Athens of the north was made secure.

Left: *Lady Stair's House, once a town mansion, now a City Museum*

Below: *View from the Camera Obscura at the top of the Royal Mile.* **Bottom right:** *The Scotch Whisky Heritage Centre, also on the Royal Mile, tells the story of Scotland's most famous export*

An Old Town tour

The best way of exploring the Old Town is on foot, starting perhaps after a castle visit or contemplation of the view from the Esplanade. Tackling the Old Town from the top has the advantage that much of the route is downhill, except for the return from a Grassmarket diversion. Sharp eyes and a little imagination are needed in order to spot small details and so to recreate the life of the Old Town. Perhaps the first detail for visitors starting high on Castlehill is a little fountain commemorating the witch-burnings which took place here between the fifteenth and seventeenth centuries. Nearby is Cannonball House, with a cannonball embedded in the gable. Many romantic tales are told about it, though it is probably only a height mark associated with Edinburgh's first piped water supply. Also close by is the Camera Obscura and Outlook Tower, whose castellated upper storeys were added in Victorian times to house the optical device which gives impressive city views when conditions are clear.

Opposite is the Scotch Whisky Heritage Centre, offering a modern 'hi-tech' experience, which includes a ride, by means of a barrel-car, through the story of whisky-making. Scotland's most famous export is presented by means of historical tableaux and sound-effects. A little way downhill, just below the junction with Johnston Terrace, is the Upper Bow, a truncated street joining from the south (on the right, looking downhill). This was once the main - and very steep - route up to the castle from the west.

Left: *The Grassmarket was one of the first market sites in Edinburgh. King James III granted this right by charter in 1477.* **Below:** *Greyfriars Kirkyard, last resting-place of many famous Scots (and one famous dog - Greyfriars Bobby)*

with its choice of shops (including one which sells nothing but hand-made brushes of all kinds). This street leads, via the West Bow, to the Grassmarket. Like the street above, called the Lawnmarket, once the site of a linen or cloth market, the Grassmarket was for centuries an important gathering-place, the chief agricultural market for the city. Now the surviving commerce is mostly of the up-market shopping variety - with one novelty a shop which specialises in selling only fossils. At the western end of the Grassmarket is a lane called the Vennel. (In fact, *vennel* is Scots for 'lane'.) This gives access to the seventeenth-century and last extension of the city's defences, Telfer's Wall.

Retracing the route to the Royal Mile, the visitor will pass a cross-shape, set in cobbles, in the centre of the Grassmarket. This was the site of the town gallows, and hence the phrase used

by a judge infamous for his harsh sentencing of the Covenanters in the Scottish religious wars of the sixteenth century: 'Let them glorify God in the Grassmarket.'

As an alternative to returning to the High Street via Victoria Street, visitors can also leave the Grassmarket to the south, up Candlemaker Row, to explore Greyfriars Kirkyard. Many famous Scots are buried there, among them the policeman master of Greyfriars Bobby. This little dog's devotion to his dead master captured the

The later development of Victoria Street sliced through it, though you can find the original route's continuation on a lower level: where it leaves the Grassmarket, a portion survives as the West Bow and is seen by looking down and right from the walkway parapet reached from the Upper Bow.

Back on the Royal Mile, Gladstone's Land is nearby on the left, while down one of the many closes in this part of the Old Town, likewise on the north side, is Lady Stair's House. This town mansion of 1622 now houses literary relics of Sir Walter Scott, Robert Louis Stevenson and Robert Burns. Another close nearby is named Brodie's Close after the infamous Deacon Brodie, who was a worthy citizen by day, carrying on a respectable trade as a locksmith. By night he turned burglar, using copies of the keys he made for unsuspecting customers. This real-life citizen, hanged in 1788, is said to have been the inspiration of Robert Louis Stevenson's tale of *Doctor Jekyll and Mr Hyde.*

If time permits, divert right at George IV Bridge to turn right again down Victoria Street,

Right: *The romance of childhood is captured at the unique and highly entertaining Museum of Childhood.*
Below: *The High Kirk of St Giles was for long the only kirk within the town walls. Mention of a church on this site was made as early as* AD*854*

hearts of many, and in consequence a doggy statue sits at the top of Candlemaker Row, where it joins George IV Bridge.

Returning to the High Street and continuing downhill, the site of the Tolbooth, the former civic centre of the old burgh, is marked out by a heart-shape set in the cobbles, a few metres down from the George IV Bridge crossroads. The heart-shape is a reference to a novel by Sir Walter Scott in which the building, now entirely vanished but for the traces in the roadway, is called the 'Heart of Midlothian'. Great changes have taken place in this area. With the Tolbooth built out into the street and almost blocking the way for centuries, the High Street was further restricted by little shops and stalls spilling out into the space all around the Tolbooth and St Giles below. This bottleneck was cleared away in the early years of the nineteenth century.

The earliest exterior part of St Giles, the High Kirk of Edinburgh, which is visible is the fifteenth-century crown spire, though some of the pillars in the nave are thought to be Norman. Such a long-established place of worship - the original building may have been replaced as early as 1120 - has seen many alterations and reconstructions over the years. As recently as 1829 the outside was 'restored', that is, the original rubble walls were covered with dull grey ashlar cladding. The Thistle Chapel within was dedicated in 1911.

Behind St Giles is Parliament House, where the Scottish Parliament met between 1639 and 1707. The building later acquired a neo-classical frontage and by that time was already the centre of the Scottish legal system, which it remains to this day. An older relic of Scottish burgh life stands nearby. The Mercat Cross, heavily restored, is still the site of royal proclamations. Opposite is the City Chambers, the seat of the civic authorities.

Lower down, just before North Bridge and South Bridge meet the High Street, is the Tron Kirk. The name comes from the salt tron which formerly stood beside it. (A tron was a beam used for weighing goods.) The kirk itself has been closed for about forty years, although plans have been suggested for its conversion to a visitor centre.

Beyond the crossroads is the Museum of Childhood, which (even without children to escort) is well worth a visit for a nostalgic look back at childhood. Opposite stands John Knox's House, only saved from demolition in the nineteenth century because of its supposed associations with Scotland's stern religious reformer. Some say that no documentary evidence exists to suggest Knox ever lived here, but the tradition is very strong and has been in print at least since 1784, when a pioneering

Left: *Canongate Kirk was built in 1688 for the congregation ousted from Holyrood's Abbey Church when King James VII converted the latter into a chapel for the Knights of the Thistle*

guidebook writer, the Honourable Mrs Murray of Kensington, visited Edinburgh and mentioned it in her subsequent guide. This information has been dutifully repeated ever since! The building dates in part from 1490 and the initials of an early owner, James Mossman, and his wife can still be seen carved on a lintel. (Mossman was goldsmith to Mary Queen of Scots and was hanged for his loyalty to her after she was forced to abandon the throne.) Below is the site of the Netherbow Port, with brass studs set into the cobbles to mark its exact location.

The Canongate continues down the hill with Moray House (1628), once a grand town house of the Dowager Countess of Home, now part of a teacher-training college. Among its other claims to fame is that it was intended to be the signing place of the Treaty of Union with England in 1707, but an angry mob, perhaps realising the treaty was a betrayal, compelled the authorities to seek refuge and sign away Scotland's future in a more secure house in another part of the Old Town. Close beside Moray House, on the other side of the High Street, is the Canongate Tolbooth, now housing 'The People's Story', one of the city's own museums, which relates how the ordinary folk of Edinburgh lived - a feature often overlooked amid grand tales of royalty and historical incident. Huntly House, opposite, built in its original form as early as 1517, is another of the city's museums. Its local history theme includes a major collection of the city's glass, pottery and silverware. Another restoration nearby is that of Acheson House (*c.* 1630), now the setting for the Scottish Craft Centre.

The Canongate Kirk, just below, has a kirkyard in which are buried several notable Scots, including the poet, Robert Fergusson, and the economist, Adam Smith. Also here is the grave of 'Clarinda', or so she was addressed by the poet, Robert Burns. She was a rich and pretty widow, Mrs Agnes MacLehose, and on one of his visits to the capital, Burns had a passionate correspondence with her. The flirtation was conducted entirely by letter, as the poet was confined to quarters with a wrenched knee!

Bottom left: *Among many famous folk buried in the Canongate kirkyard is 'Clarinda', Mrs MacLehose, a rich widow who held a passionate correspondence with the poet Robert Burns*

Below: *White Horse Close is typical of the restorations which have breathed life back into the lower portion of the Royal Mile.* **Bottom:** *The Palace of Holyroodhouse grew from the guest-house of the now-ruined Holyrood Abbey*

Still lower down the Canongate is White Horse Close, the point from which stage-coaches for London departed in the days before Regent Road was built. Regent Road is the broad thoroughfare which is the eastward continuation of Princes Street, beyond Waterloo Place, whose construction took traffic away from the foot of the Royal Mile. This meant that the Old Town no longer had a main route running into it, which in turn pushed the area around the Canongate into a decline in the nineteenth century - and into this decline likewise sank the Palace of Holyroodhouse.

In a sense, the full stop to the long statement on Scotland's story contained within the Old Town and the Royal Mile, the Palace of Holyroodhouse evolved from the guest-house of Holyrood Abbey, now only a ruined shell. The present palace building was founded by King James IV at the end of the fifteenth century. Construction continued under his son, King James V, though the work was damaged during the episode of English devastation of parts of Scotland known as the 'rough wooing'. (This was King Henry VIII's not over-subtle attempt in the 1540s to marry off his young son to the infant Mary Queen of Scots in the hope of uniting the two kingdoms.)

After 1603 and the Union of the Crowns, King James VI enjoyed the increased power and prestige of the English court, of which he was King James I, so much, that he returned to Scotland only once and briefly in 1617, preferring to rule from a distance. Holyroodhouse became redundant as a royal residence. After being damaged by fire in 1650, while occupied by Cromwell's troops, it was rebuilt on the orders of King Charles II in 1671. The architect, Sir William Bruce, added a matching tower to the original King James Tower and linked the two with a set of apartments to create the façade which is seen today. Hardly used, the palace again fell into disrepair, until Queen Victoria's enthusiasm for Scottish themes led to further restoration. Beyond the palace are the former hunting grounds of the Scottish monarchy, now Holyrood Park.

Left: *Princes Street from Calton Hill, perhaps one of Edinburgh's most famous views.* **Bottom left:** *The National Gallery of Scotland occupies a conspicuous site on the Mound, overlooked by Edinburgh Castle*

Below: *Perhaps one of Edinburgh's most distinctive landmarks, the Gothic fantasy of the Scott Monument recalls Sir Walter Scott, one of Scotland's greatest novelists and champions.* **Bottom:** *Planned as an exclusive residential street, Princes Street soon gave way to commerce and is now a main shopping street*

A New Town tour

As the Mound, the snaking ramp which offers such fine vistas of Princes Street and its gardens, was intended to link the Old and New Towns, it is appropriate to start a New Town tour from it. The lower end of the Mound is dominated by the architect Playfair's work in the form of the National Gallery of Scotland and, facing Princes Street, the Royal Scottish Academy. Turning right onto Princes Street, the visitor finds the Scott Monument dominating the skyline ahead. This spectacular departure from the restraint and order of the neoclassicists is a Gothic fantasy of spires and statues, with a marble figure of Scott and his favourite dog ensconced within. There are 287 steps to the top, with breathtaking views as a reward for effort. Beyond the shrine to Scotland's champion, on the other side of the road at the east end of Princes Street is Register House, custom-built as Scotland's archive. Part of its funding came from the sale of estates forfeited after the last Jacobite rebellions by their Jacobite owners.

Beyond Princes Street it is worth walking along the handsome sweep of Waterloo Place,

Left: *The National Monument was intended to commemorate the dead of the Napoleonic Wars, but funds ran out and work stopped in 1829.* **Bottom left:** *St Andrew Square, the easternmost of the two squares which formed part of James Craig's original plan for the New Town*

over the Regent Arch (designed as a war memorial), to reach the curious collection of monuments on Calton Hill. On top, the miscellany includes the Gothic-flavoured Old Observatory (by James Craig) and the New Observatory, conforming to neoclassical taste with its cruciform shape and pillared symmetry. It is another of Playfair's designs. He was also responsible for the adjacent monument to his uncle, John Playfair, a noted mathematician and philosopher, and for the reproduction of the monument to Lysicrates in Athens, which serves as a memorial to the philosopher Dugald Stewart. Overlooking the steep drop to Waterloo Place below, the Nelson Monument is like an upturned telescope in shape and hence instantly recognisable. Even more conspicuous are the impressive columns of what was intended to be the National Monument to the dead of the Napoleonic Wars. Planned as a copy of the Parthenon in Athens, it was never completed, as funds ran out. In consequence, it is sometimes called Scotland's Disgrace. Also from the Calton Hill vantage-

point can be seen the memorials in the New Calton Burial Ground, notably the Martyr's Monument, a pencil-thin column commemorating five men who were sentenced to transportation for their dangerous views in 1793. They had advocated that everyone should have a vote. Nearby is the 1930s St Andrew's House, the administrative headquarters of the Scottish Office. It was built on the site of the former Calton Jail, of which only the Governor's House remains, recognisable by its crenellated parapet and its cliff-edge setting overlooking Waverley Station.

Return to Princes Street (or cut through the St James Centre, built on a part of the New Town which was demolished) to turn north and reach St Andrew Square, one of the original two squares in the symmetrical plan for the first phase of the New Town. Perhaps the most notable building in this now greatly altered square is the headquarters of the Bank of Scotland. This was built as the home of the wealthy and influential baronet, Sir Lawrence Dundas. The original plan had specified a church on this spot, matching the

Centre left: *West Register House was opened in 1814 as St George's Church, but was converted in 1971 to a public record office. The congregation united with that of St Andrew's Church, towards the east end of George Street.* **Below:** *St Andrew's Church in George Street*

Below: *The north side of Charlotte Square, one of the finest pieces of civic architecture anywhere in Europe.* **Bottom:** *The National Trust for Scotland has restored the Georgian House, which is intended to recreate life in the New Town at the time when it was originally built*

one that was eventually built at the far end of the plan: the former St George's in Charlotte Square (now West Register House, instantly recognisable by its copper dome). However, the well-connected Dundas managed to acquire the site for his own house. The building which should have stood here can be seen a little way along George Street to the west - the handsome St Andrew's Church.

Other notable features of George Street include the statue of King George IV. This recalls his visit to Edinburgh in 1822 - an event which was organised by Sir Walter Scott and was

remarkable for the resulting revival of tartan, which Sir Walter insisted upon as part of the pageantry. It was in the Assembly Rooms, a little further on, that Scott finally acknowledged authorship of *Waverley*, the novel which was originally published anonymously and which became a bestseller in its day. Charlotte Square, full of character, is the impressive west end of

George Street. The block on the north side of the square, with its magnificent palace front, hardly altered since it was built in the last years of the eighteenth century, was to the plan of Robert Adam, though he did not live to see his design realised. It is still considered to be one of the finest pieces of civic architecture to be seen anywhere in Europe. At the Georgian House (no. 7), the National Trust for Scotland has recreated life as it was enjoyed by a well-to-do family in Georgian times, when the square was new. This is the highlight of any New Town exploration, though the excursion may be continued downhill to the north and west to discover, for example, the environs of Moray Place or, a little further on, the leafy riverside walkways of the Water of Leith.

Below: *Craigmillar Castle*

Places to visit

This is just a selection of the many places of interest Edinburgh has to offer. Details are correct at the time of writing, but may be changed.

City Arts Centre
Market Street (Tel: 031 225 2424).
Open Jun-Sept, Mon-Sat 10-6, Sun during Edinburgh Festival 2-5; Oct-May, Mon-Sat 10-5. Usually free admission.

Craigmillar Castle
(Tel: 031 661 4445). $3\frac{1}{2}$ miles south-east of city centre on A68. Open Apr-Sept, Mon-Sat 9.30-7, Sun 2-7; Oct-Mar, Mon-Sat 9.30-4, Sun 2-4 (closed Thurs pm, and Fri in winter).
Admission charge.

Edinburgh Butterfly and Insect World
Melville Nursery, Lasswade (Tel: 031 663 4932). 5 miles south of Edinburgh on A7 towards Dalkeith. Open 25 Mar-31 Oct, daily 10-3.30. Admission charge.

Edinburgh Castle
Castle Rock, Royal Mile (Tel: 031 225 9846). Tickets available: Apr-Sept, Mon-Sat 9.30-5.05, Sun 11-5.05; Oct-Mar, Mon-Sat 9.30-4.20, Sun 12.30-3.35. Castle closes 45 minutes later. Admission charge.

Edinburgh Zoo
Corstorphine Road (Tel: 031 334 9171). Open summer, Mon-Sat 9.00-6.00, Sun 9.30-6.00; winter, Mon-Sat 9.00-5.00 (or dusk if earlier), Sun 9.30-5.00 (or dusk if earlier). Admission charge.

Georgian House
7 Charlotte Square (Tel: 031 225 2160).
Open Apr-Oct, Mon-Sat 10-5, Sun 2-5.
Admission charge.

Gladstone's Land
477b Lawnmarket, Royal Mile (Tel: 031 226 5856). Open Apr-Oct, Mon-Sat 10-5, Sun 2-5. Admission charge.

Greyfriars Bobby
Corner of George IV Bridge and Candlemaker Row.

Huntly House
Canongate, Royal Mile (Tel: 031 225 2424). Open Jun-Sept, Mon-Sat 10-6; Oct-May, Mon-Sat 10-3. Sun during Festival 2-5. Admission free.

John Knox's House
45 High Street, Royal Mile (Tel: 031 556 9579/2647). Open Mon-Sat 10-5 (last entry 4.30). Admission charge.

Lady Stair's House
Off Lawnmarket, Royal Mile (Tel: 031 225 2424). Open Jun-Sept, weekdays 10-6; Oct-May, weekdays 10-5. Sun during Festival 2-5. Admission free.

Museum of Childhood
High Street, Royal Mile (Tel: 031 225 2424). Open Jun-Sept, weekdays 10-6; Oct-May, weekdays 10-5; Sun during Festival 2-5. Admission free.

National Gallery of Scotland
The Mound (Tel: 031 556 8921).
Open Mon-Sat 10-5, Sun 2-5. Admission free.